# Mistakes Men Make

# That *Women* Hate

*Also By* **Kenneth Karpinski**

*The Winner's Style*, Acropolis Books, 1986

*Red Socks Don't Work*, Impact Publications, 1994

# Mistakes Men Make

# That *Women* Hate

# 101 STYLE TIPS FOR Men

*By*

## Kenneth Karpinski

CAPITAL
BOOKS, INC.
*Sterling, Virginia*

**Copyright (c) 2003 by Kenneth Karpinski**

CAPITAL BOOKS, INC.
P.O. BOX 605
HERNDON, VIRGINIA 20172-0605
ISBN 1-931868-46-8 (alk.paper)


**Library of Congress Cataloging-in-Publication Data**

Karpinski, Kenneth J., 1948
    Mistakes men make that women hate : 101 style tips for men /
Kenneth Karpinski—1st ed.
        p. cm.
    ISBN 1-931868-46-8 (alk. paper)
        1. Men's clothing. 2. Fashion. 3. Grooming for men   I. Title.

TT618. K367 2003
646'.32—dc21

                                        2003067389


Printed in the United States of America on acid-free paper that meets the American National Standards Institute Z39-48 Standard.

First Edition
10 9 8 7 6 5 4 3 2 1

To Judy,

the most stylish editor an author could hope for.

# Introduction

Have you ever wanted to tell a friend how to improve his image, but you just didn't feel comfortable delivering the message? Wherever I am or whatever I am doing, when I pose this question, the tales pour out. At the merest mention of the subject, everyone within earshot wants to tell me about someone whom they wish they could tell to fix his appearance because it's sabotaging his effectiveness.

*Continued*

Of course, most people remain silent, either because they feel they don't know the person well enough to tell him something as personal as how to dress, or because the "mistake" seems so obvious that they assume he should know better. If you are one of the silent ones, this book of mistakes men make and the tips to correct them is a way to help out your friends and loved ones.

And should you be the recipient of this book, consider it your best friend. It will tell you what your best friend can't—or won't.

# Pocket Full of Pens

(MORE THAN TWO IS THE INTERNATIONAL NERD SYMBOL.)

But make sure the pen you carry is a good one. A quality pen is a sure sign of a cultivated style. When doing business, it is a compliment to be handed a fine pen with which to sign.

# Tinted Glasses Indoors

(THEY MAKE YOU APPEAR INSINCERE; YOU DON'T NEED THE HANDICAP.)

People want to see your eyes in order to feel comfortable with you. Being able to look someone in the eye is a way of determining trustworthiness.

# Too Long Necktie

(AS LONG AS IT DOESN'T INTERFERE WITH THE ORDERLY OPERATION OF YOUR ZIPPER, IT'S NOT TOO BAD.)

If you wear a belt, try to have the tie end within the width of the belt. If you choose to wear suspenders, a little more leeway is allowed.

# Unbuttoned or Missing Button-Down Shirt Buttons

(BUTTONS ARE THERE FOR A REASON, SO USE THEM OR SWITCH
TO A STRAIGHT COLLAR.)

Some people prefer a button-down collar because it keeps the points down and neatly in place. Not using the buttons suggests carelessness or lack of understanding their purpose.

# Jacket Collar Not Anchoring

(YOUR JACKET SHOULDN'T LOOK LIKE IT IS STANDING UP BEFORE YOU DO.)

There shouldn't be any space between your shirt collar and the collar of your jacket. If there is, something is wrong: fit, model, or manufacturer's style is the probable cause.

# Alligator Tie Clips/Bar

(THEY DO KEEP YOUR TIE OUT OF MOVING MACHINERY, BUT THEY'RE A BIT OLD-FASHIONED.)

Today's style is looser and more relaxed. Slide the narrow end of the tie through the label loop and let it move freely.

# Old, Worn-Out, Broken-Down but Comfortable Shoes

### (COMFY DOES NOT MEAN DEAD AND GONE.)

A gentleman's dress shoe can be either a slip-on or lace-up.

Whichever you choose they must be (1) dark in color,

(2) made of leather, (3) highly polished, and (4) well maintained.

# Dark Dress Socks with Shorts

(THIS LOOK IS OKAY ONLY IF YOU'RE IN BERMUDA OR
WEAR THE SOCKS OVER THE CALF.)

The more casual the shorts the less appropriate

it is to wear dark, ankle-length dress socks.

# Ornate Belt Buckles

(IF IT RESEMBLES AN INCA SUN GOD, YOU SHOULDN'T BE
WEARING IT TO WORK.)

A simple silver- or gold-colored belt buckle will go perfectly
in every dressy situation. Save your rodeo trophy buckle
for the weekends—unless you work at a ranch.

# Spitting in Public

(UNLESS YOU ARE CHOKING, IT IS HIGHLY GROSS.)

The necessity to spit is a learned habit that can
and should be unlearned.

# Seven Hairs across the Top

(IF YOU ARE LOSING YOUR HAIR, ADMIT IT. MAKING THOSE SEVEN HAIRS
WORK OVERTIME ISN'T GOING TO FOOL ANYONE.)

Take care of the hair you do have without resorting to attempts
at camouflage or redirection. Moving the part or combing the
hair against the natural growth pattern are tricks that are
always more obvious than you think. A naturally receding
hairline is nothing to be ashamed of.

# Wrinkling across the Front

(HORIZONTAL, ACCORDION CREASES SAY "TOO TIGHT.")

Wrinkles are an almost inevitable condition when wearing plain-front trousers. Being certain they are not too snug across the hips will help; wearing pleated-front trousers is even better.

# Shirt Tail Pulling Out

(WHY LOOK HALF UNDRESSED?)

Rubber stays, sewn into the waistband of the pants, can help. Many manufacturers make a longer tail, but in extreme situations a made-to-measure or custom shirt may be needed for the additional length.

# Business Shoes with Sports Clothes

(MIXED SIGNALS SAY "OUT OF TOUCH," "CARELESS," OR
"I FORGOT MY GYM BAG.")

A business shoe is designed to balance the heaviness of a suit of clothes and will look awkward with a pair of khakis and a knit shirt.

# Cheap Necktie

(NECKTIES MADE OF INEXPENSIVE FABRICS ARE NEVER A BARGAIN;
PEOPLE CAN TELL EVEN FROM A DISTANCE.)

Colors and patterns on polyester don't look as rich or softly elegant as they do on silk. Few man-made fabrics compress as well as silk, so the knot will not be as compact or well formed.

# Sport Socks with a Suit

### (BULKY, FUZZY SOCKS BELONG IN THE GYM.)

If the socks are navy, black, or gray and your pants are long

enough, you can probably get away with this one. Better to

buy yourself some thin dress socks, though.

# Vent Pulling Open in Back

(NOT THE TIME OR WAY TO SHOW OFF YOUR REAR END.)

Jackets come with vents in one of three styles: single vent, side vent, and closed vent. The vent should hang straight down with no pulling or opening.

# Black Socks Worn with Sandals

(IF YOUR TENDER TOES CHAFE, SKIP THE SANDALS.)

Bare feet and sandals go together. If the occasion is appropriate for wearing sandals, then wear them, but skip the socks.

# 100 Decibel Nose Blowing

(SOUNDING LIKE A MOOSE IN HEAT ONLY ATTRACTS ANOTHER MOOSE.)

Excusing yourself to a more private location before you begin will be appreciated by all within earshot.

# Fu Manchu Mustache

(DROOPY, DANGLING FACIAL HAIR CAN SCARE PEOPLE.)

A mustache should extend only a little past the corners of the mouth. The more it goes past and down, the more sinister and unprofessional it becomes.

# Narrow End Longer Than the Wide End

(IF YOU WANT TO LOOK LIKE YOU DON'T HAVE A CLUE, THIS WILL DO IT.)

The wide end of the tie must be longer than the narrow end.
The small loop of fabric on the back of the wide end is meant
to hold the narrow end in place.

# Too Much Jewelry

(THE "RULE OF SEVEN" APPLIES TO MEN AS WELL AS TO WOMEN.)

Simply stated, the Rule of Seven says, "You should not have more than seven points of interest on your body at one time." A point of interest is anything that in and of itself will draw attention, like a ring, belt buckle, or highly decorated shirt.

# Shirt Front Pulling Open

(TOO TIGHT, TOO SMALL—NOBODY WANTS TO SEE YOUR
UNDERSHIRT OR HAIRY STOMACH.)

If your body is no longer trim, don't try to wear a tapered
shirt. If regular cut or "gentleman's fit" shirts are too full,
have them adjusted with darts to eliminate the excess.

# Unlined, Light-Colored Pants

(SHOWING THE OUTLINE OF YOUR RED BIKINI BRIEFS ISN'T SEXY.)

A partial lining or slightly heavier fabric will prevent this, as will avoiding too-tight pants and opting for boxer shorts when wearing light-colored, summer-weight pants.

# Grandfather Clock on Your Wrist

(NO BELLS, WHISTLES, OR SIGNAL FLARES TO MARK
THE QUARTER HOUR, PLEASE.)

A classic watch is an investment that will pay dividends for
many years to come. If cost is a problem, there are excellent
reconditioned and replica watches available.

# Broken, Patched Laces

(IF YOU'RE JUST TOO STRONG, GET HELP WHEN TYING YOUR SHOES.)

When buying a pair of lace-up shoes, purchase an extra pair of laces and keep them in the car's glove compartment or at home, in case of a break.

# Jacket Not Long Enough

(ALWAYS COVER YOUR SEAT.)

To check for correct length, (1) measure from the nape of the neck to the floor and divide by two; or (2) with your arms by your side, curl up your fingers—the skirt of the jacket should just rest in the curl of your fingers.

# Gaudy Monograms

(IF THEY CAN BE READ FROM MORE THAN FIVE FEET AWAY,
THEY ARE TOO BIG.)

In the beginning monograms were ways to identify one
person's property from another's. Small, subtle initials
on the pocket or chest are dignified and proper.

# Dressy Tie with a Casual Shirt

(THIS COMBINATION COMPLETELY DEFEATS THE PURPOSE—WHY BOTHER?)

Knits of cotton or wool and many club or conversational ties
go perfectly with a casual denim or patterned shirt. Stay
away from shiny silks or dressy patterns like foulards or dots.

# Ponytailed Hair

(ONLY THE MOST ARTISTIC NEED APPLY.)

This tactic rarely makes you look younger. A ponytail combined with a naturally receding hairline makes you look as though your hair is slipping backward.

# Bubbling, Wrinkled Front of Chest

(A JACKET SHOULD NOT APPEAR TO HAVE A TROPICAL DISEASE.)

The front layers of some jackets are held together by a process called fusing. High heat can sometimes cause this to break down and look bubbly. When a jacket reaches this point, it cannot be fixed, so discard it.

# Bloody Shirt Collar

(LOOKING LIKE A FAILED SUICIDE ATTEMPT IS DISTRACTING.)

Nicks and cuts sometimes happen. A styptic pencil can save
you from leaving little spots of blood on your shirt collar.
Shaving well in advance of getting dressed also will allow
you to clot before you button up.

# Black Socks with Everything

(WELL, THEY TOLD US NOT TO WEAR WHITE SOCKS WITH A SUIT.)

There is no rule that says you must wear black socks. Wear gray socks with gray suits and navy with navy. Subtle patterns are in fashion, so give them a try.

# Loud, Plaid, Double-Knit Pants

(THESE CAME IN AND WENT OUT IN THE SIXTIES—ENOUGH SAID.)

At one time these pants were thought to go with everything; in fact, they really went with nothing. If you own them, don't worry about them coming back in style—they won't.

# Dress Shoes That Aren't Black, Brown, or Cordovan

### (ELVIS HAD HIS BLUE SUEDES. YOU'RE NOT ELVIS.)

Black goes with black, navy, and gray; brown goes with all of the earth tones like brown, tan, and olive; cordovan goes with just about everything—a great travel shoe.

# Pierced Body Parts

(NOSE, LIP, OR TONGUE—NO WAY JOSÉ.)

Pirates wore earrings to signify the survival of a shipwreck.

I have no idea what a pierced tongue says.

# Dirty Eyeglasses

(THE EYES ARE WINDOWS TO YOUR SOUL.)

When someone speaks with you they want to look you in the eye. It is impossible to ignore unsightly smears and unidentifiable crud that come between your eyes and theirs.

# Necktie Pressed to Death by an Iron

### (A FLAT TIE HAS NO STYLE.)

A tie is meant to be folded and tacked together. Pressing removes all of its life and causes the lining to show through the silk. Light steaming will remove most wrinkles.

# Poorly Chosen Eyeglass Frames

(ONE STYLE DOES *NOT* FIT ALL.)

Follow this four-step checklist:

(1) choose frames that complement the shape of your face,

(2) small metal frames are more elegant than plastic,

(3) pupils should be in the center of the frame, and

(4) tops of the frames should be close to the natural eyebrows.

# Melted-in Collar Stays

(PLASTIC MELTS WHEN PRESSED!)

Remove the plastic collar stays before sending shirts to the laundry to avoid having them melt and show through the layers of fabric on the collar points. Metal stays might not melt, but they will leave marks when pressed over.

# Jacket Fabric Out of Season

(LIKE WEARING MITTENS IN JULY, IT MAKES PEOPLE WONDER.)

If your clothing needs to span the seasons, try to buy year-round fabrics in natural fibers. Nontextured and midweight-wool will easily keep you comfortable and looking appropriate ten months of the year.

# Stapled Pant Cuffs

(IMAGINE SETTING OFF AN AIRPORT METAL DETECTOR BECAUSE OF THIS.)

If you haven't done this, you probably know someone who has.
Keep a small mending kit of needle and thread in the car, at
the office, and at home. Be very smart and thread the needles
in advance, so that in an emergency all you need to do is
apply a quick stitch.

# Penny Loafers with a Suit

(SAVE THE PENNIES AND BUY A PAIR OF DRESS SHOES.)

Casual footwear with dress clothing is inconsistent and makes you look like an amateur. If a pair of slip-ons seems okay with a casual shirt and a pair of cotton pants, they are probably too casual to wear with a suit.

# Exposing Your Shins

(*PLEASE* DON'T DO THIS. WEAR SOCKS THAT ARE LONG ENOUGH.)

Midcalf and over-the-calf socks are more comfortable than ever before, so try a pair of the new, mostly natural fiber socks available today. They are worth the price.

# Bent and Soiled Business Cards

(YOUR CALLING CARD SHOULD NOT SAY "CARELESS.")

Use a case designed to carry business cards; it keeps them fresh and always available to exchange. After all, you don't want to appear as though exchanging a business card is a unique experience for you.

# Belted Trench Coats

(DON'T BELT THEM.)

Wear the belt knotted in back or with the ends stuffed into the pockets. It looks too stiff to belt the coat "properly."

# Five o'clock Shadow

(YOU CANNOT BE TAKEN SERIOUSLY IF YOU NEED A SHAVE.)

Daily shaving is a necessity for everyone over twenty-one. If your beard grows very heavily, a late afternoon touch-up with a cordless electric shaver may be needed for evening appointments.

# Clip-on Ties

(UNLESS THERE IS A REAL DANGER, LEARN HOW TO TIE A NECKTIE.)

Men working around fast-moving machinery and in law enforcement do wear these for a reason, but they're the only ones. There are only three ways to tie a necktie: Windsor, half-Windsor, and four-in-hand; of the three the four-in-hand goes with the most shirt collar styles.

# Pockets Full of Stuff

### (REMEMBER CAPTAIN KANGAROO.)

If you must carry a lot of stuff around with you, at least spread it around by using all the pockets in the man's average suit. There are twelve in all, if you count the two small change pockets inside the right-hand pant and jacket pockets.

# Pilling Collar Fabric

(THESE TINY FUZZ BALLS SCREAM "INEXPENSIVE.")

Most often seen where the collar comes in contact with the neck, fabric pills are the result of friction and cannot be removed effectively. They make a shirt look cheap and worn out.

# Gunslinger Trousers

(FOUR INCHES BELOW THE NAVEL IS A NO-NO, IF YOU ARE OVER
TWENTY-ONE YEARS OLD.)

Dress trousers are not meant to be worn like jeans. The pleats
will blouse out, your gut will hang over, and the seat of your
pants will hang out of place if worn too low. Belt them within
an inch of your navel.

# Bloodshot Eyes

(CLOSE YOUR EYES BEFORE YOU BLEED TO DEATH.)

Use one of the many over-the-counter products available to help remove redness and make you appear more alert and up to the challenges of the day.

# Clip-on Suspenders

(CLIPS ARE OKAY FOR LITTLE KID'S MITTENS, BUT NOT FOR
GROWN MEN'S PANTS.)

Button-on braces have six points of support to help keep your
pants up; clip-ons have only three. The metal alligator clips
don't look dressy enough to work well with a suit.

# Shabby Briefcase

(YOU CAN'T DRIVE YOUR SPORTSCAR INTO A BUSINESS MEETING.)

Because it functions as a portable office, your briefcase must reflect an impeccable sense of style any time you leave the office. A briefcase says so much about you. Buy the best leather you can afford. It will serve you well for years and even improve with age.

# Polishing Your Shoes with a Hershey® Bar and a Brick

(TRY A PROFESSIONAL SHOESHINE, A MAN'S LAST LUXURY.)

People make judgments about you based on your shoes. Take time to care for your shoes properly; not only will they look better, they'll also last longer.

# High-Water Pants

(FORGET THE JOHNSTOWN FLOODS—PANTS MUST COME DOWN
TO COVER YOUR SOCKS.)

The bottom of your pants must reach your shoe tops. If you choose to wear cuffs they must come down and rest on the shoe.

# Collar Too Loose

(IT MAY BE COMFORTABLE, BUT IT MAKES YOU LOOK SICKLY.)

One finger should fit comfortably between your collar

and your neck.

# Jacket Too Small

(JUST BECAUSE YOU CAN BUTTON IT DOESN'T MEAN IT FITS.)

If there are horizontal lines, if the vent pulls open, if the lapels bow out, or if the front button could become a lethal weapon should you sneeze, it is just too small.

# Stained Necktie

(YESTERDAY'S LUNCH MENU SHOULD NOT BE VISIBLE.)

Very light dabbing with a gentle spot remover is all you can do. Some water spots can be removed by gently rubbing the spot along the grain of the tie with the silk of the narrow end. Dry-cleaning is rarely successful. Choose wisely from the menu or befriend a necktie salesman.

# Tie Pins and Tacks

(PUTTING A HOLE IN A SEVENTY-FIVE-DOLLAR PIECE OF SILK IS FOOLISH.)

Because of the hole, you are forced to wear the pin in the same place every time. After a while the tie begins to look like part of a uniform.

# Overstuffed Wallets

(WEDGING SOMETHING THE SIZE OF A DELI SANDWICH INTO YOUR REAR
POCKET DOES NOTHING FOR YOUR IMAGE.)

Most men need to trim down the contents of their wallets.

A realistic review of the items will reveal a lot of things

not necessary every day.

# Fishy or Viselike Handshake

### (YUCK AND OUCH!)

The correct way to shake hands is by joining hands web to web, holding firmly, not squeezing, and pumping no more than three times.

# Unkempt Beard and/or Mustache

(THE ABSENT-MINDED PROFESSOR LOOK DOESN'T INSPIRE
CONFIDENCE IN ANYONE.)

There is nothing wrong with choosing to wear facial hair, but
make certain to trim, shampoo, and comb it often to maintain
a professional appearance.

# Lobster Bib Ties

(THE WIDTH OF YOUR TIE SHOULD MATCH THE WIDTH OF YOUR LAPEL.)

Compare the widest part of your tie with the widest part of your notched lapel; they should be virtually the same. This comparison does not work well with a peaked lapel.

# Collar Too Tight

(IF THE BUTTON IS IN DANGER OF BECOMING A LETHAL PROJECTILE...)

Buttoning the top button of your shirt should not cause your face to turn red or stop you from breathing. Sometimes collars shrink and sometimes necks get bigger. Don't continue to wear an uncomfortable shirt collar. (And yes, people notice when you knot your tie over an unbuttoned collar.)

# Lapel Popping

(WATCH OUT FOR A PLACE FOR BUNNIES TO HIDE.)

The lapels of a jacket should conform to the contours of your chest. When the lapels bow away from your chest, your jacket is either the wrong model or it is too small through the chest.

# Fear of Pleats

("I CAN'T WEAR PLEATS; THEY MAKE ME LOOK FAT.")

Anyone can wear pleats if the pants fit properly. Give them a try; they're going to be around a long time. Remember, pleats are a matter of function, not fashion. When you sit down and expand, they expand along with you.

# Black Shoes with Tan Pants

(IT SHOWS NO SEMBLANCE OF A THOUGHT PROCESS.)

Any shade of brown, cordovan, or earth tone will work better.

# Rain/Trench Coat Too Short

(ONLY COLUMBO CAN DO THIS.)

A coat should always fall below your knees. Midcalf length
or slightly longer is very acceptable.

# Wally the Walrus Mustache

(IT LOOKS CUDDLY AND FUN BUT IT CAN BECOME A SOUP-STRAINER.)

Trimming a mustache at the top of your upper lip prevents a lot of problems that can arise when eating or drinking. A dense mustache can trap particles of food that could get gamey over the course of a day.

# Overstuffed Suitcase on a Business Trip

(IF YOU NEED THAT MUCH STUFF, TAKE TWO.)

It takes a lot of ironing to free smashed-in clothing from
the ravages brought on by trying to fit too many garments
in one bag just so you can carry it on.

# Ink-Stained Pocket

(NOBODY WILL THINK IT IS CHINESE CALLIGRAPHY.)

The quicker you can act on this the better. Getting to a professional cleaner as soon as possible and letting the experts do their best is your only hope.

# Tie Too Short

(THIS IS NEITHER ARBITRARY NOR NEGOTIABLE.)

Your tie must reach your beltline. Too short a tie makes you look silly, unsophisticated, and out of touch. If you want to look like a rube that just fell off a turnip truck, this will do it.

# Suspenders Worn with a Belt

(YIKES! UNLESS YOU ARE TREMENDOUSLY INSECURE—
NEVER, NEVER, NEVER.)

They both are used for the same purpose — to keep your
pants up — so the duplication of effort is excessive.

# Unbuttoned Double-Breasted Jacket

(ONLY DAVID LETTERMAN HAS GOTTEN AWAY WITH THIS—
YOU'RE NOT DAVE.)

Double-breasted jackets are made to be worn buttoned.
They don't hang properly when they are not.

# Any Extreme Hairstyle

(SPELLING OUT YOUR NAME ON THE BACK OF YOUR SKULL
WON'T GET YOU MANY BUSINESS CALLS.)

If your hairstyle is making a statement, I guarantee that
it isn't saying anything positive about you. Keep it short to
medium length with no buzz cuts or Mohawks allowed.

# Really Unusual Appointment Calendar

(NO FLOWERS, PAISLEY, OR CARTOON ANIMALS WITH VELCRO CLOSURE.)

A small, unobtrusive calendar that can be carried comfortably when you are out of the office is all you need. Try a Personal Digital Assistant (PDA). They hold more information, are smaller and come in lots of colors.

# Three-Inch-Thick, Thirty-Pound Folio

### (NOBODY IS THAT BUSY! GET A GRIP ON REALITY.)

Most people don't need to carry more than a month or two of appointments with them at a time. Carrying more than one book in a briefcase is far better than trying to keep everything in one book. Imagine what you would have to do to replace it if it were lost!

# Fraying Sleeves or Collar on Shirt

### (IF IT'S WORN OUT, THROW IT OUT.)

Continual rubbing of the ever-growing beard on the front of the neck and hair on the back of the neck against the collar and entering the pockets thousands of times while wearing a wristwatch will wear out the fabric.

# Trousers Worn Too High

(A PANT'S WAIST SHOULD BE CLOSER TO YOUR HIPS THAN YOUR NECK.)

There is a reason cartoonists use this image as shorthand for "ignorant bumpkin" or "oblivious geezer".... A man's dress trousers are meant to be worn on the waist, with the band at approximately the level of the navel.

# Tie Clips and Tie Tacks

(THERE ARE BETTER WAYS TO KEEP YOUR TIE OUT OF YOUR SOUP.)

While they are still being worn, they appear dated. However,
tie chains are making a comeback and will do the job of
keeping your tie in place without damaging the fabric.

# Alligators Nipping at Your Heels

(RUN-DOWN SAYS "OUT OF LUCK.")

If you can fit the eraser end of a pencil under your heel,

it needs repair.

# Necktie Knot the Size of Cleveland

(IT'S A WONDERFUL CITY, MY SISTER LIVES THERE,
BUT YOU GET THE IDEA.)

Strive for a knot that fits proportionally within
the collar opening of the shirt you are wearing.

# Missing Shirt Collar Stays

(A FLYAWAY COLLAR SAYS, "I DON'T CARE" OR "I'M UNAWARE.")

Stays keep the points of a shirt collar down and in place,
positioned over the necktie. Really good shirt laundries
remove them before laundering and return them to you
in a small envelope when you pick up your shirts.

# Shoulder-Length Hair

(NOT A GOOD IDEA UNLESS YOU'RE APPEARING ON THE
COVER OF A ROMANCE NOVEL.)

Outside of the scholastic and artistic communities long hair
does not fit in. Besides not looking consistent when dressing
up, constantly brushing it out of your face is distracting.

# Unwashed, Greasy Hair

(THIS IS ONE TIME THAT BEING A QUART LOW IS GOOD.)

Using high-quality shampoos and conditioners every
day is necessary if you are active or have oily hair.

# Cellular Phones in Restaurants

## (IS THAT YOURS OR MINE?)

Keep it in your briefcase — use it in private. If the call is that important you shouldn't be sharing it with the world. If it isn't, end the call quickly, promising to return it later.

# Traveling with a Monster Suitcase

(STOP SWEATING AND SWEARING—SUPPORT A SKYCAP.)

It is impossible to look cool, calm, and collected while dragging eighty pounds of dead weight through twelve miles of airport corridors. Hire help, or travel with two smaller bags.

# T-shirts at the Office

(YOU MAY THINK IT'S COMFORTABLE, BUT "BOOGIE 'TIL YOU PUKE"
T-SHIRTS DON'T WORK. PERIOD.)

T-shirts are not nearly as dressy as shirts with a collar.
Button-front and polo styles will always look better than
a T-shirt alone. Try wearing a brightly colored T-shirt
under a button-front shirt to show a little personality.

# Collar Bar with a Button-Down Shirt

### (YOU DON'T NEED BOTH TO KEEP A COLLAR UNDER CONTROL.)

A collar bar is considered dressy, a button-down is casual. The mix of styles makes you look like you don't know what you're doing.

# Matching Tie and Pocket Square Set

(MATCHY-POO IS NOT FOR YOU.)

The pattern in the pocket square should coordinate but not be identical to the tie. Choose a color or two in the tie and bring them out in the colors of the pocket square.

# Do-It-Yourself Eyeglass Repairs

(IT HAS NEVER BEEN DONE SUCCESSFULLY AND YOU WON'T BE THE FIRST.)

Paper clips or staples where the hinges should be and tape on the bridge or temples must be avoided at all costs. With the opening of eyewear superstores all over the country, there is no need for a long-term "emergency" repair.

# Fun Ties in a Serious Situation

(DON'T MAKE A STATEMENT YOU MAY WISH TO TAKE BACK LATER.)

Match the tone of your tie to the situation. If the pattern of a tie

takes attention away from you or your message it is too much.

There is a difference between individuality and distracting.

# Gaudy Cuff Links

(IF YOU CAN'T LIFT YOUR ARM WITHOUT HELP, THEY ARE TOO BIG.)

French cuffs are becoming increasingly popular, so cuff links are a must. If metal or semiprecious stones are not for you, try silk cuff knots for understated elegance.

# Shorts and a T-shirt at Work

("BUSINESS CASUAL" IS NOT AN EXCUSE FOR BEING A SLOB.)

If you would seriously consider cutting the grass or moving a refrigerator in them, your clothes are not appropriate for an office environment.

# Chewing Gum or Tobacco

(YOUR MOTHER TOLD YOU NOT TO DO THIS IN PUBLIC, REMEMBER?)

Both habits will do nothing to improve your image, unless you are auditioning for the road company of "Lil' Abner."

# Too-Long Shirt Sleeves

(YOUR SLEEVES SHOULD EXTEND ONLY ONE-HALF INCH
BEYOND YOUR JACKET.)

A shirt sleeve should end at the point where your wrist
and hand come together.

# Barely There Mustache

### (IF IT DOESN'T WANT TO GROW, THERE MAY BE A REASON.)

In a cosmetic attempt to appear older, some men try to grow a mustache. But if it is too thin or light colored it will defeat your purposes and actually exaggerate a youthful face. Enjoy your youth; other men are paying thousands of dollars to get that look back.

# See-Through Dress Shirt Fabrics

(VERY FEW WANT TO SEE THROUGH TO THE REAL YOU.)

Look in a mirror—can you see a shadow or texture through your shirt? Sheer, light-colored dress shirts should be backed up with a white T-shirt, preferably a crew neck, to provide an opaque background and to absorb perspiration.

# Belt Too Small

(SQUEEZING EXCESS FLESH UP AND OUT IS REVERSE CAMOUFLAGE.)

Wearing the correct size belt has a slimming effect. Don't worry about the number stamped or sewn inside. Manufacturers all cut a little differently, so try on several belts and buy the one that is most comfortable. As a bonus, it will also look the best.

# Comb Visible in a Pocket

(PEOPLE WON'T THINK YOU ARE A WELL-GROOMED PERSON—HONEST!)

Having a small pocket comb tucked away is a great idea, but carrying it so it is visible or pulling your comb out in public is not acceptable.

# Index

# Index *Continued*